Lingering Laments

Lea Batara

BookLeaf
Publishing

Presentation by *BookLeaf Publishing*

Web: www.bookleafpub.com

E-mail: info@bookleafpub.com

ISBN: 9789395969628

First edition 2022

DEDICATION

Lola, let's look at the stars and talk to the moon tonight.

The one where I moved on

I can't help but check my phone
every now and then –
and wonder if you've sent me something,
anything, again.

As always there is nothing new
you'd asked if I'm ok,
as if you hadn't took my heart
and drove, with it, away.

Up I scroll, reread our texts,
searching for some hidden clue.
There's nothing there it's so mundane
your empty I love you's.

It's been – what – maybe a jillion days
Since I saw your name pop up;
onto the banner of my phone –
Is ignoring it enough?

I lied when I said "now and then"
I checked for the first time today.
The first time since you messaged me
and asked if I'm ok.

Sometimes, for meter's sake I force a rhyme,
even if it doesn't fit.
Maybe that's what I did to both of us –
and that's what led to this.

In a depressive cycle

Laying in bed
With nothing to do
I go to the window
And hope the sky's blue

With birds flying everywhere
And sun bursting through
The glass of the windowpane
Still dripping dew -

Instead it's raining and windy
And there's even snow too
No, the weather hasn't changed
even when the sky's blue

Now the day's a whole waste -
What am - I - supposed to do?
Guess I'll just go back to

Laying in bed
With the covers over my head
Wishing the day's over
Because I want something new.

Is this it? right now?

To the nights I can't remember
And the days I can't forget
You work so ironically, capturing yet
withholding it all
Or maybe that's just human nature
The way we experience your movement.

We think we know you
That we measure you according to our actions
Thoughts
Feelings
But the truth is we don't

You're unbiased
Unforgiving
Constant
There's no speeding up or slowing down
Or going back, reaching ahead
(at least not in this dimension)
You're simple, yet difficult to deal with
Everyone handles your essence differently
Very few have mastered your influence
And those who live by your movement alone
don't live at all
Letting your passing dictate their actions.

I don't blame them though
It's hard not to
When we spend your majority asking
What are you doing right now?

I'm scared of dying* with an asterisk*

Sitting on the bus watching the world
outside blur into horizontal lines
I wonder what would happen if the bus crashed
And I die

(*but only me and no one else everyone else is
safe and unharmed)

I don't even feel fazed by this for me
And what's even scarier is that the
More I think about it the
More I don't mind.

(*So long as no one else is hurt and sad by this.)

Ponderings

How do you move on
after bad things happen?

How does everyone expect you to move on
and be "normal" again?

How do you act like nothing happened
when everyone's already moved on?

How do you speak out again
when you're terrified of the outcomes?

How do you navigate the unspoken
conversations between us, like a dance where
i'm expected to lead but can't?

Why do terrible things happen to the good
people in my life
(and how do I help them)?

Why do I feel so guilty for hitting up my friends
and family even when I'm so proud of them and
happy for them but I bring down the vibes
because I'm still
working on myself?

Kaibigan

The ones who see me listening to my sad playlist
and hit me up to check on me
The ones who reply to my stories and chat
The ones who send me songs or links or articles
or posts or tweets and say "thought of you"
The ones who always apologize for not replying
right away even tho they know I'll say "don't
worry about it"
The ones who send me relentless messages or
stay on call for a while because they know I
need company right now
The ones who drop everything to call me or
come over when I'm in distress
The ones who share their day, passions, love, life
with me, go off babes!

I don't need to hear from you every day
But when I do, I cherish it always

Spiraling

When you're stuck in a hole and hate it
But you like it
What does that mean?
Being alone
Surrounded by darkness
Nothingness
What does that mean?
I may despise my thoughts
But I can't deny how much I adore myself
My thoughts are so genius it makes me ill
What does that mean?
I am a smart person.
I am a waste of talent.
I know I'm intelligent.
I am a waste of space.
I know I'm capable.
I am a waste of breath.
I know I can take over the world.
What does that mean?
I won't.
Because I'm worthless, useless, and
I'm not going to be able to do any of it.
I can't so bad I want to cry
Sometimes all I do is cry.
What does that mean though?
Let's dive into it
- again

Bojack

Why do I do this to myself
I'm on a path to be my truest self
Find my inner peace
See clarity
Nirvana or
Whatever
But I can't help scratch an itch
One at the back of my head

The very back

And it's saying
"Stop trying u stupid piece of shit"
"No one likes u"
"Why r u even texting them"
"Why do u even do that"
"why ru here"

The irony it all is
I suck, I mean
It sucks

Just like bojack does at making headlines.

I love my support system

I can't
Wrap
My head
Around
How you -
A complex individual, with your own
Thoughts
Feelings
Problems
Hobbies
Friends
Lives -
Can spare me the precious moments
Of your time
To tell me it's ok;
Keep going;
You can do it;
You are loved;
Especially at times when I'm so low
I'm just beating myself up.
Why are you
Spending this time
On me
I so clearly don't deserve shit

I so clearly need to change myself
I feel so guilty
I don't want to let you -
A caring, thoughtful human being -
Down.
Abandon all hope
Warns the tattoo on my forehead
Being a constant burden like
Those things swallowing anything around it
So why do you -
A busy,
Productive,
Self-made
Human -
Care about me?
Why don't I
Care about me
More?
I'm learning
Taking inspiration from
You.

Ponderings the sequel

Sometimes it's all too much. How can I ensure my family knows and understands how much I love and cherish them and everything they've done? How do I do that when our past is so complex? How do I show my love in its purest form in general? How do I show my friends? I don't wanna show it to my friends either, but I want my family to know that I've forgiven them all, always. Idk how. I get so emotional about it because I don't want them to think or feel like they messed up or something's off. I love them so so so much. I feel like I'm back in school here when I'd get a bad mark and I don't know how to tell my parents I was truly trying my best.

Maybe that's it.

To take all the mental gibberish and lock it in a jar and store it somewhere safe where it can't hurt anyone and just let the rest of me live. Let my body be free and what couldn't I do then? What could I accomplish without this constant bombardment of thoughts and reminders to stay present be present or it'll all fall apart again.

And I can feel it trying to fall apart again I know
I'm in a better place and I've held it all off for so
long what is wrong with me it's because I know
I don't feel great but it'll pass it always passes
we all pass but not NOW not YET it's not my
decision? it's a moment not forever but why
does it always come back? will it ever stop?

Clock thoughts I'd like to turn off

Tick tock
Tick
Breathe in
Tock
Breathe out
Tick
Blinding light
Tock
Rush of air
Tick
Screaming
Tock

Tick tock
It's a cycle

Tick tock
Never ending

Tick tock
Well I'd like to hope it ends
Tick
But lots of people are afraid
Tock
Of the end
Tick
I'm so in my head
Tock

I scare myself
Tick
I just want to quiet these voices
Tock
Thoughts
Tick
SHUT
Tock
UP
Tick tock
Shutupshutupshutup
Tick
Here I am again
Tock
Alone?
Tick
Never
Tock
I'm always here
Tick
Can't escape
Tock
Myself
Tick
be nice
Tock
To yourself
Tick
Be kind in your words
Tock
To yourself
Tick

I hate you
Tock
I say to myself
Tick
I love you
Tock
I reply
Tick
I don't care at all
Tock
I answer
Tick
You've attempted so many times
Tock
I counter
Tick
Just nike already
Tick
I mock
Tock
You coward
Tick
Shut the fuck up already
Tock
I retort
Tick
To the voices in my head
Tock
Least there's one thing in common
Tick
They just want
Tock

Me
Tick
To
Tock
Tick

I'm trying to get better

To you who sees me
For who I am
What I am
I'm so sorry
I'm so grateful

To you who sees me
And still believes
It's gonna get better
I'm so sorry
I'm so grateful

I see you
I'm grateful
I'm trying

A circle vs. a spiral

cant start so I'll put on my favourite study music and oop an ad maybe I should give them the time of day but then I remember it's my time of day and so I skip and increase the volume okay I'm back let's write about the way this scene made me feel but what's the word for when you think you're really getting to know someone but really you're projecting your feelings/desires onto them like a host body ooh how do I type that out that's crazy right I should just rephrase that whole thing to be more palatable okay here I go and wow that sounds pretentious and far off my intended meaning I should take a break this is hard right now and a little too much for me to handle let's pause and regroup for a quick second 'til I feel ready to do it for real for real I heard theres a new episode out let's race to it and while it's loading I might as well start eating my food because nothing bad ever happens when I'm eating so let's ramp up all the endorphins and double dose that dopamine and I'll be right back on track when I'm finished this walloping packed punch of serotonin and happiness this is amazing. and now I'm back to work and I—

return to my work, terrified of the ongoing progress
I've made. If this isn't good what's the point of 4
years in uni? Because I made friends and had fun and
learned how to get a job where's that job now?
What's your point? Everyone switches career paths?
But this is what you fought for. So? I don't like it
anymore it brings me stress. Besides, I can barely do
it. Can barely do it or you're so afraid of failure you
won't do it so you don't even give yourself the chance
and avoid the disappointment before you can even
try? Yes, all of it. So what are you gonna do? Keep
taking 'breaks' in disguise as productive steps
towards your goal? Even when you know you've
already used them as productive steps before? I don't
know. What do you want to do? I don't know. What
can you do? I actually don't know. Me neither.

Social interactions are hard

As much as I love to write
I am terrified of it
The way it solidifies my mistakes (read:
thoughts)
For which I've yet to forgive myself so
It's scary not being
Able to be comfortable
Around others

How I've hurt others
Friends family people I love
Myself especially
The pain of not being able to perfectly translate
your intentions with words alone

Between gratitude and forgiveness
Maybe internalized toxicity
That depresses me
But are we really all that pointless?
Meaningless?
Do we really have to make up meaning about
each other
To be considered into our lives?
Or are we all just meant to be used by each other
Endlessly

Discarded and picked up
Until they're not useful anymore?
Or am I the devil projecting,
a vessel for vicious validation
of my own self hatred to overcome?
How do I prove my use?
My own worth?
Does it matter?
Do I need it to matter?
Is that enough?

Keep moving forward

Maybe to move forward and seek distractions is the
way it'll always be,
and some people are better at focusing on the
distractions than the emotions they elicit. Are all
experiences distractions?
Is life a never ending checklist of tasks to get through
to attain, what,
Heaven?
Nirvana?
Peace?
Fulfillment?

The burden of simply being is more so
an art,
a struggle,
a way of
living that requires tremendous
energy, or maybe a lack
of self-awareness? Fascinating
how much experience and emotion and intelligence
and introspection
seduces the mind
and
controls the soul.

Or, then again, maybe I'm mad, stricken by mental
illness and "normal" people don't think this way.
"Normal" people don't have these thoughts, they

don't question their successes, their failures, their
goals, their experiences, their emotions, themselves.
Maybe they simply do, and be done.
I want that.

I hate that I love that I hate that I love how intelligent
I think I am, how clumsily self-aware I am, how
blindly (not) aware of my surroundings I am. To
know you're alive is to bite the head off a shark or
whatever that one old person said or carved into a
tree.
I know, and within all that knowing
is the truth that ultimately, I do
not know anything at all.

I am limited, I know little in the grand scheme of
things and the little I do know haunts me, burdens
me, so how could I possibly think of knowing more?

The vastness should make me feel better but the
paradoxical nature of it all confuses me more. Will it
be like this until I end? I don't know. I want to be
satisfied with not knowing.
So on I push.
And the weary mind does its best to keep up.

Imposter syndrome, meet intrusive thoughts

It feels like a weight scrunching and pulling down on
the centre of my forehead
All the skin is converging to the middle of my
forehead dragging it forward
The realization is physical
The realization that people don't know anyone
They don't know what you're going through, just like
you don't know what they are either
You choose how much to divulge
Even if you're unsure how—

Staring out the window actively listening to my
friends convo from the front of the car I get caught in
a spiral of thoughts and unable to have anything
relevant to contribute to their conversation - car
crashes and sibling woes - and, well I do have
everything to contribute I have anecdotes but I am
too scared to speak because they hurt to bring up and
then it hurts me that I feel like I can't even express
that to my own friends because I don't wanna be sad
and bring down the vibes and I don't wanna be
someone people don't wanna hang out with because I
don't wanna be me and I don't know what to do or
say and
now I've waited too long I've been so silent I clear
my throat to make sure they know I'm here still I was

coughing so much at work why can't I even muster a
cough
now I need to let my friends know I love and
appreciate them being here with me and hanging out I
miss them and that I'm scared and hurting and I'm
not fun to be around right now but they make such a
good time and I don't know how to acknowledge that
without sounding selfish because I need them and
love them and I don't wanna be alone right
now.
Maybe I don't know how to be alone. Properly. So I
stare out the window as their convo drifts on and I
think and think and think and think about how indeed
to be present I need to be mindful we're all gonna die
and we never know and we can't turn back time in
this reality and we can't hold onto this moment right
now forever so I need to make my presence known
but I don't want it to be this sorry pathetic sad shell
of a person I am right
now and so I interject abruptly
"Does anyone else think that aliens have already
infiltrated the planet?"

And in the pregnant, slightly surprised pause I add
"sorry to interrupt I got lost in my thoughts and that
came out."

This is why I have no friends.

Upside down arch reactor

Tony stark was a genius
That's as plain as day
Thanks for creating iron man
You're welcome, claimed RDJ

You built a whole reactor
To react to things it touches
Connections stretched like tentacles
Or really are they crutches?

An arc reactor - fancy!
That's one cool cat you are
To turn into a reactor so you
Are never far
From danger

You're a good reactor,
That's how you can ignore
Your own "problems"
Simply by making someone else's problems yours.
You built the best reactor
You're just like me you see
You're such a great reactor
You don't know how to simply be.

Affirmations (I know, I know, sigh)

May each time you breathe you inhale gratitude and
exhale apathy.
May each moment fully immerse you and be infinite.
May the good and bad moments create harmony.
May any guilt become compassion.
May the universe continuously bring you prosperity,
balance and healing.

May we have the strength to keep moving forward
and to give ourselves space to reset and relax.

May we pursue our dreams and remember to
celebrate all our achievements.

May we continue learning, expanding our horizons to
include different perspectives and in turn learning
about ourselves and how we love and live.

May we fall in love with what's in front of us instead
of potential.
May we find love in every moment even when it
seems impossible.

May we fall deeper, love harder and be kinder to
ourselves because Lord knows what we've through in
the past year alone and how it'll shape us this year.
May your love for yourself guide you and let you put
faith in others, carefully.

Double tap to claim!

Amen.

Ha sorry I still don't know how to end this it sounds
like a prayer.

She was a sk8r boi

Lines
Like very crisp fives
Hold on Holden
Watch me die
Rapture seems impossible
Catch her in the lie

She just wants to hold your hand and
All those cliche parts
Where they meet cute
And then we root
For their friendship love and growth
Together
But alas

It seems so far
The distance between
Their own selves and to each other
One day they'll meet where they belong

And pick right back up from so long
And all the time that gone and passed
Will feel like it'll never last

Because she can't escape her mind
It fleets and flutters losing time
And he can't seem to shake his woes
What complimentary opposing foes
They get along too well it's true

They love who they are together too
But even that is not enough
In a world where things are rough
And being united can be tough
When opposing forces can't work together

Catching your dues
Morning hues
Blue and pink and orange and violet
Streak my face and the world
With a lens that
You knew walking was the Best Part

Of my time spent working Nights
It's little things I think
That make me like us
Or maybe it's just forcing a narrative again

I'm sorry it hurts to read. Healing sucks huh.

Ponderings again

Is this part of self-discovery always full of questions?

Why have I, even as a child, questioned myself about who I am? Why do I not know? Is it because I do not know what I'm doing here? Meaning, purpose, function all following existence? Or is it preceding? Or is it because I do know who I am? And I refuse to listen sometimes. I refuse to be mindful. Because I know when I am mindful all these questions fade and I'm left with my mind, cleared, knowing I am the same as everyone else, floating in a boundless space, hurtling towards time and the end inevitable.

I'm complacent and furious with myself and my surroundings. I'm doing too much all at once. Oh to be at least a little less self aware. Is that vain? Maybe.

I wish I didn't know that even amongst friends and family I only have myself. I wish that even if I knew that, I would be better to them. To me. Even though I am treating them the way I'd like to be treated, the best way I can, giving as much as I'm able. I wish I could unload this introspection onto someone who wasn't me, but is me enough to comprehend.

It's frustrating and paradoxical that other people struggle in similar yet unique ways because we are all alike, forever intertwining, sonder
Yet we are not comparable because of our uniqueness, because we are relative to ourselves - at least that's what we say when we want to feel better.

"At least I'm not doing x like y is" even without the comparison to others the comparison to ourselves hurts too, even if we don't mean to, or at least, that's how I feel: "at least Ik I've done x before" so why can't I do it again? Because that was a past you, a different you shaped by different times and experiences.

Is that supposed to make me feel better? Is that proof enough of my own strength? I think it could be. I think it helps sometimes. Writing helps a lot. So does water.So does being around safe company. So does lying in bed. So does sleeping. So does meditating. So does consuming things - music, art, videos, food - that help me forget. So does consuming things that help me challenge myself, thoughts, beliefs values.

At the end of the day I love. I love a cliche I love
being cringe I love being corny.

I love the magic my dad and I share in manifesting
our futures now. I love how mom is so
unconditionally caring and strong and brave and
persevering. I love the way my sisters are growing
and learning and trying. I love the way you try. I love
the way you show love and intimacy. I love the way
you show fear and grief and sadness. I love that
you've let me into your journey, even a lil.
I love that this list won't end.

To my happiness

Sometimes I feel like I've exhausted all the happiness I've got.

I know how that sounds. Especially coming from me.

So I cling to embrace the moments that make me feel good, happy wholeheartedly because it's a fluke right? It won't happen ever again right? Nothing is promised. Nothing is certain. I don't know when I'll ever feel this way again; I just have to embrace it or watch it flee. Or both.
So I *cling* to this feeling of picking flowers and listening to my favourite songs and reading my favourite books even though I know it won't last.

I keep a list of moments and feelings now. I hope it helps:
- When he drank from the fountain and then kissed me
- When we sat at the park and lounged à la Seurat (on a Sun too)
- When we spotted the tree and admired her beauty (first of many that summa)
- When we peered at some rocks and I fell in (twice)
- When we decided to pick up litter on my mental health (hot girl) walks
- When we went to convocation (hi mom & dad!)

When we sang you happy birthday!and blew out candles and tala wanted to as well

When we are all right now on new adventures with different people - we are exploring the world!

When we went camping and there was no service no wifi no concept of time (and no shrimp in the shop duh)

When we said "love u" on the phone the first time (platonic power!)

When she gave me her yellow lenses and I got so see the world thru her eyes for a mo'

When my dad and I shared our stories of magic - he manifested buying a whole house!

When my mom continues to take care of us and herself after such tiring hours at work

When my dad holds car litterers accountable by honking at them

When my dad can identify all the birds as we travel

When my sister tries and tries again and GETS it (I love the way you all try)

When we discovered three-seeded mercuries (and the synchronicity of reaching full circle)

Stay a while, there will be more.

ACKNOWLEDGEMENTS

To my family, friends, and colleagues (you know who you are!) thank you for your kindness and patience.

Adenieke, Ahmed, Al, Alex V, Alex W, Alejandro, Bernice, Emilie, Frances, Fred, Juhi, Kyler, Lana, Lauren, Liz, Mariam, Melissa, Mila, Moe, Nadine, Rhea, Rosemary, Sarah, Sher, Zike, Zora - you already know words only begin to capture the amount of love and gratitude I have for such incredibly supportive friendships. I am beyond honoured, proud, and humbled to call you among my closest friends.

Mrs. Mandarino - I did it! Thank you for always believing.

Mom, Dad, Issa, Laurie, Tala - I love you all more than you can know. Thank you for unconditional love and support as we grow and flourish together.

You all inspire me so much,
To grow
To learn
To embrace new experiences.
Thanks for sticking through my ups and downs and everything in between.